# The Transparent Life
## &
# Your Eternal Destiny

# The Transparent Life
## &
# Your Eternal Destiny

*Brian Gaither*

XULON PRESS

Xulon Press
2301 Lucien Way #415
Maitland, FL 32751
407.339.4217
www.xulonpress.com

© 2020 by Brian Gaither

All rights reserved solely by the author. The author guarantees all contents are original and do not infringe upon the legal rights of any other person or work. No part of this book may be reproduced in any form without the permission of the author. The views expressed in this book are not necessarily those of the publisher.

Unless otherwise indicated, Scripture quotations taken from the New King James Version (NKJV). Copyright © 1982 by Thomas Nelson, Inc. Used by permission. All rights reserved.

Scripture quotations taken from the Holy Bible, New International Version (NIV). Copyright © 1973, 1978, 1984, 2011 by Biblica, Inc.™. Used by permission. All rights reserved.

Scripture quotations taken from the Holy Bible, New Living Translation (NLT). Copyright ©1996, 2004, 2007 by Tyndale House Foundation. Used by permission of Tyndale House Publishers, Inc.

Scripture quotations taken from the Amplified Bible (AMP). Copyright © 1954, 1958, 1962, 1964, 1965, 1987 by The Lockman Foundation. Used by permission. All rights reserved.

Printed in the United States of America.

ISBN-13: 978-1-6312-9774-8
Ebook: ISBN-13: 978-1-6312-9775-5

This book is dedicated to my lovely wife, LaWanna, and my two children, Nigel and Brianna. Your steadfast love for and patience with me is indeed a sign and reality of God's love.

Special thanks to Bishop Beechard Moorefield and Bishop James C Hash, men of high integrity and faithful teachers of the Word of God, helping to shape the man I am becoming.

# Table of Contents

Introduction . . . . . . . . . . . . . . . . . . . . . . . . . . . . . . ix
Chapter 1  The Fall – The Power of a Decision . . . . . . 1
Chapter 2  Don't Hide From Truth . . . . . . . . . . . . . . . 9
Chapter 3  A Better Lens . . . . . . . . . . . . . . . . . . . . . . 15
Chapter 4  New Image. . . . . . . . . . . . . . . . . . . . . . . . 23
Chapter 5  Shut Up, Snake. . . . . . . . . . . . . . . . . . . . . 29
Chapter 6  Wake Up. . . . . . . . . . . . . . . . . . . . . . . . . . 35
Chapter 7  See HIM! . . . . . . . . . . . . . . . . . . . . . . . . . 39
Chapter 8  God Is Not a Man . . . . . . . . . . . . . . . . . . 45
Chapter 9  I See YOU! . . . . . . . . . . . . . . . . . . . . . . . . 51
Chapter 10  Yes, I AM Weak . . . . . . . . . . . . . . . . . . . 57
Chapter 11  It's Not Their Fault. . . . . . . . . . . . . . . . . 63
Chapter 12  I Need Comfort . . . . . . . . . . . . . . . . . . . 67
Chapter 13  The Real Conversation With God . . . . . 73
Chapter 14  Love's Got You . . . . . . . . . . . . . . . . . . . . 79
Chapter 15  More Than a Conqueror . . . . . . . . . . . . 83

# Introduction

As we begin this book, I first want to clarify that I am not a motivational speaker. I am an inspired minister of the gospel and its Truth. This book will challenge you and stretch you while you examine yourself by the light of God's Word. I have come to understand in my own life that the Truth of God can make you uncomfortable, but I know when you do what He says, it will save you, deliver you, redeem you, and God will forgive you and take complete care of you. We all fight the same fight, saved or not, and that fight is the daily choice of following the direction of God or the plans of man.

My plan in life was to become a professional athlete. For as long as I can remember, basketball and football have played a critical role in my life. My plan was to get drafted by a great Division I college, notably the University of Notre Dame for football or the University of North Carolina for basketball, going on to become a star player and have a signature shoe and my face on a Wheaties cereal box. Raised in a Christian home, my mother and father did all they could to provide for my siblings and me, but we weren't wealthy. Sports became my getaway—my fallback. High School scholastics opened the door to a football scholarship to Western Carolina University as a quarterback. There I met my wife and learned some valuable lessons about decision making.

For me, college was just a way to play professional football. I did what was needed to play on the field. At the time, it worked, but as I look back, I wish I respected my free educational opportunity more. Nevertheless, I graduated with a business degree.

Upon graduation, I saw another part of my dream come to pass when the National Football League's Baltimore Ravens contacted me as a free agent in 2002. My life was changed: I had reached the pinnacle of my life. I was given the world as I knew it, but it was short-lived. I was eventually released from the organization at the end of training camp, which created a significant void in my life. I thought that another door would surely open—that another team would give me a chance—but after a few workouts and a trip to Canada, it became evident that my dream may not come true.

My athletic ability had measured my identity in life. For the first time, I was not good enough in my mind; I felt rejected by the very thing I thought I was born to do. I fell into a terrible depression. I returned home and moved back in with my parents.

I began attending my childhood church and at my mom's request, served on the worship team. Later, I served as a youth leader alongside my wife. I did all this while battling significant bouts of rejection and condemnation, which manifested in loneliness, a loss of purpose, and depression. I received my first job through a church member who knew I had a need and connected me with a local mobile home dealer. There I sold single-wide, double-wide, and modular homes.

*Introduction*

While I valued work and was thankful for the opportunity, you can imagine the level of confidence I had during this time. But I was committed to showing up each day and giving my best. I met some great people and began to realize I had a gift with people and for bringing people together, which opened the door to my next job in sales as an assistant manager and suit sales associate at a large retail store. I still battled depression. I was married, expecting my first child, served in the worship and youth ministries, and had accepted a position on our church board.

Life appeared to be going in the right direction, but I still saw myself as an athlete. I was passing the time and making the best of the hand I had been dealt. But God had another plan. While maintaining my job in suit sales, I desired a career in banking. I filled out application after application without a call or interview. One day at work, a gentleman with a very particular style came in. He loved suits with vests. I made it my mission to show him everything we had that met his need, even locating things online and at other locations. The service I provided inspired him to buy three suits. During our conversation, he mentioned that he was a branch manager of a credit union. And not just any branch—the brand headquarters a few miles down the road. He was appreciative of the work I had done to serve his needs and asked if I had ever considered working in the financial arena. Wow!

I immediately jumped to attention and let him know that I had applied with his credit union, along with many other banks, but I had not received a response. He told me to bring my resume to work in two days when he would return for his altered suits. He would personally make sure that human resources received it and that I would get an interview. I worked for the credit union for seven years; life was beginning to make a little sense. I started to believe that I had found my second-best purpose in life: meeting the needs of people by providing financial services that would improve their lives. Awesome, right? But God wasn't done. He began to work on my heart concerning ministry. There was a burden and a call to pastor—something in which I wanted no part. I still warred with my own identity. I wasn't qualified to tell anyone else how to live.

I was a failure working his way back into things. But God won. Within a year, I had confessed the calling to pastor to my then-pastor, Beechard Moorefield, and he and I began a four-year transition to becoming the pastor of the church I was attending. I am thankful to him for guiding me through the process and entrance into ministry.

So, what happened with the feeling and lack of purpose? God began a healing process, which is the power of this book. I had to come to grips with certain facets of my life and look at the idols I had developed, the selfish ambitions I had created for myself, and the things in which I had begun to place my identity. I am not saying I have perfected these emotions now—I war within myself daily as you do—but, I am learning tools of transparency before God that bring tremendous strength to my weaknesses. Ministry, as a leader, has revealed even more vulnerabilities in my life: things I have faced with the help of the Holy Spirit and the Word of God, coupled with the right support circle. God's desire for us is total victory and success, but these areas must be adequately defined.

*Introduction*

The need to be successful and productive can be swallowed up in performance and vanity. Chasing an idea of success can make us vulnerable, and without proper guidance, we can find ourselves in an endless cycle of heartbreak.

God wants better for our lives. Realizing this requires a willing and diligent search in the Word of God to locate Kingdom principles. We will discuss Kingdom principles in this book, but for now, let us set the foundation for becoming a transparent person. Everyone has a desire to live better—a desire to see an increase, for a better relationship or job—and all these things are in the mind of God for you, but you must submit your plan to His.

Proverbs 14:12, New International Version (NIV), says, "There is a way that appears to be right, but in the end, it leads to death." The power of this scripture rests in the heart of man.

Every man produces from the heart. "A good man brings good things out of the good stored up in him, and an evil man brings evil things out of the evil stored up in him" (Matthew 12:35, NIV). Your life is a direct connection to what you choose to believe and what you think is a direct influence of what you have sown in your heart by what you see and hear. "The eye is the lamp of the body. If your eyes are healthy, your whole body will be full of light." (Matthew 6:22 NIV). Furthermore, Romans 10:17 NIV, "Consequently, faith comes from hearing the message, and the message is heard through the word about Christ."

God has a way of blessing you that this natural world is not aware of, but it requires you to seek the Kingdom first (Matthew 6:33). What we must understand is that there are two different systems in operation. We, as natural people, are influenced by two spiritual Kingdoms: the Kingdom of Light and the Kingdom of darkness. These realms of the spirit speak to the decisions we make and the results we see. The Kingdom of darkness operates on self-ambition, self-motivation, and self-production, and with that, you depend on yourself to produce a life beyond your power to deliver. Why? Because God's made you for Him. He wanted to be our sole provider, and our identity and success would work through His provision and direction. Jeremiah 17:5-9 NIV says:

"This is what the Lord says: "Cursed is the one who trusts in man, who draws strength from mere flesh and whose heart turns away from the Lord. That person will be like a bush in the wastelands; They will not see prosperity when it comes. They will dwell in the parched places of the desert, in a salt land where no one lives. But blessed is the one who trusts in the Lord, whose confidence is in him. They will be like a tree planted by the water that sends out its roots by the stream. It does not fear when heat comes; its leaves are always green. It has no worries in a year of drought and never fails to bear fruit. "The heart is deceitful above all things and beyond cure. Who can understand it?"

When we try to create a life based on our ideas and strategies, we destroy the very thing God has had for us all along. The greatest thief of God's promises is man's agenda. This book take's the light that is God's Word and exposes the path that you, dear readers, are on. There is no greater discerner to the Truth outside of the Spirit of God fed by the Word of God. Read with your heart open, and your ears and eyes targeted on God's best and take this journey into whom you were purposed to be.

*Introduction*

"What is mankind that you are mindful of them, human beings that you care for them?" (Psalm 8:4 NIV). The creation story in a word is awesome—to look at God's work and His majesty, brilliance, and creativity. Yet His very best came right out of Himself. Nothing in creation was empowered to have god-like dominion until God spoke to His man in Genesis 1:26 NIV. " Then God said, "Let us make mankind in our image, in our likeness, so that they may rule over the fish in the sea and the birds in the sky, over the livestock and all the wild animals, and over all the creatures that move along the ground. " These Words were the Word of blessing breathed into the DNA of humankind. This decree separated humanity from every other created thing and gave him dominion over them, which is very significant in the light of living a transparent life. Genesis 2:25 reads, " Adam and his wife were both naked, and they felt no shame." Notice they were naked and without shame; they were open to God.

*Chapter 1*

# The Fall – The Power of a Decision

**Genesis 3:19 (NIV)**

"By the sweat of your brow
you will eat your food
until you return to the ground,
since from it you were taken;
for dust you are
and to dust, you will return."

Decisions. We all must make them, and every decision we make impacts the next step we take or the future we live in. Adam, the first man, had a decision to make, and he made one. Made in the image of God, he carried the Spirit of God and the authority to carry out God's Word by The Blessing pronounced over him by God.

## Genesis 1:28 King James Version (KJV)

"And God blessed them, and God said unto them, **be fruitful, and multiply, and replenish the earth, and subdue it: and have dominion over the fish of the sea, and over the fowl of the air, and over every living thing that moveth upon the earth."**

These words were the words of dominion on the earth. God's man and woman were not created to be dominated by anything. The man had the power to use God's authority. The spirit and mind of the man were filled with the goodness of God. His purpose was to create a beautiful world. There was one thing God told him not to do—not to eat of the tree in the middle of the garden.

## Genesis 2:15-17 New Living Translation (NLT)

'**The LORD God placed the man in the Garden of Eden to tend and watch over it. But the LORD God warned him, 'You may freely eat the fruit of every tree in the garden—except the tree of the knowledge of good and evil. If you eat its fruit, you are sure to die.'**

The Word to Adam was don't eat the fruit from the tree. His disobedience led to death. Allow me to bring context to the word *death*. This death was not physical; it was spiritual death. Upon eating the fruit, the spirit of the man would be disconnected from the source of his life, which was God. God is life, and to be disconnecting from Him is to be connected to sure death.

This command was not a command to bring burden but to keep Adam and eventually Eve in the way of life. The source of their wisdom did not need to come from a tree—they had within them the life of God, and God Himself came and walked with them in the cool of the day. What more do you need, right? A life so grand could not have a negative attribute; one would think, but wherever the promise of God is, there will be a counterfeit option. Satan brought the woman an offer at the tree—questioning her, creating a discouragement in her identity.

### Genesis 3:1-7 (NIV)

"Now the serpent was craftier than any of the wild animals the LORD God had made. He said to the woman, **"Did God really say, 'You must not eat from any tree in the garden'?"** The woman said to the serpent, "We may eat fruit from the trees in the garden, [3] **but God did say, 'You must not eat fruit from the tree that is in the middle of the garden, and you must not touch it, or you will die.'"** "You will not certainly die," the serpent said to the woman. "For God knows that when you eat from it, your eyes will be opened, and you will be like God, knowing good and evil."** When the woman saw that the **fruit of the tree was good for food and**

**pleasing to the eye, and desirable for gaining wisdom, she took some and ate it. She also gave some to her husband, who was with her, and he ate it. Then the eyes of both of them were opened, and they realized they were naked; so, they sewed fig leaves together and made coverings for themselves."**

Notice the enemy came in and did not blatantly expose his agenda. He offered intriguing questions that caused Adam and Eve to question everything they were told. He first made them doubt God's Word. "Did God really say?" Have you ever felt like the Word of God did not apply to you? Like what you read was for other people but did not include you? The enemy will try to discredit God's word in our lives to fulfill his agenda. Beloved reader, what God spoke in His Word is for you. Every promise perfected in Christ is for you: healing, provision, deliverance, salvation—it is for you. Let nothing talk you out of that. God is not a respecter of any person; He is a respecter of our faith. If you can believe Him, it is possible.

Next, the enemy tried to get them to question their identity and what God purposed them to do. "For God knows that when you eat from it, your eyes will be opened, and you will be like God, knowing good and evil." Words of doubt attack your identity and suggest that maybe God did not give you everything. You might think there are things still lacking in your life—areas of inadequacy. This is a lie of the enemy to lead you to look toward other things to fill the void that only God can fill. Knowing good and evil was something God could have shown Adam and Eve as they continued to walk with Him. The ability to come to this knowledge did not have to be the result of direct disobedience. It could have been learned the right way, walking in a relationship with God and inquiring of Him.

I now recognize many times in my life that I allowed my desires for things popular in the world to manipulate my perspective. Many times, the desire to fit in with my peers caused me to forsake my walk with God. Sports became my greatest desire. Achieving a level of respect among my peers became the focus rather than fulfilling God's purpose for my life. There were many times when I felt the tug of the Holy Spirit calling me away from particular gatherings or events in which there were drugs and alcohol, but in those moments, I found fitting in more pleasurable than pleasing God. It was pleasurable at the moment, but just like many others do, I felt the condemnation of not resisting temptation. I always promised never to put myself in those positions again, only to return to the same situation repeatedly. The approval of people was my weakness. I didn't realize that God had already accepted me.

Notice what happened when they began to entertain the words of a snake. The very thing they were told not to eat became something that looked ideal for consumption. May I add that every tree that God made was good for food, to look upon it, and to eat from it. These trees were at their disposal, but they entertained the voice of deception. Pride is the result of fraud. When we begin to consider thoughts that go against the Word of God, we take on a mind of self-righteousness. This mentality causes you to look at forbidden things as the ideal option. We all face these challenges daily. The problem is knowing what is right and standing on it, rather than entertaining thoughts that try to exalt themselves above the knowledge of Christ. The longer we entertain the wrong ideas, the more desirable the ideas become. The origin of these thoughts— both good and bad—is the spirit realm. They desire to work through us what is right or what is wrong in accordance with God's plan.

There are two Kingdoms. The Kingdom of light, which is founded on obedience, and the kingdom of darkness, which is based on disobedience. Compliance is the life of Christ, while rebellion is linked to the life of Adam. See Romans 5:12-20.

Thank God for Jesus. Because of Him, we do not have to live under the disobedience of Adam, which leads to sin and that sin to death. We can live through the obedience of Christ Jesus, which leads to freedom and freedom to life. According to I Timothy 2:13-14, Adam was aware of His position; therefore, he was not deceived by the serpent. But Eve was deceived. This decision changed the course of humanity's life. The curse came as an act of the flesh or personal decision. With the curse came the work of toiling.

> **Genesis 3:19 (NIV) "By the sweat of your brow you will eat your food until you return to the ground since from it you were taken; for dust you are and to dust, you will return."**

Man would work hard until he died without God's Word to produce for him. Everything he received, he would have to work hard to get. Any crops he grew would come through the contention of weeds and corrupted soil. Now, if we are honest with ourselves, many of the things we get today come through hard work.

*The Fall – The Power Of A Decision*

The world is filled with people trying to "make a living." The truth is that your livelihood is supposed to come through the Word of God. He desires us to take Him at His Word and keep it so that we can prove to ourselves and the world that His Word is true. In my life, I leaned on my physical abilities to get me to my destiny. My natural ability was my work. My ability to charm and win people over was the gift I used to get ahead. I was going to use it to achieve my professional career. And it almost worked. Yet, when I came to an end, I found I wasn't enough.

What do you depend on to make you whole or complete? What goals have you set that you have already planned out in your mind? Once again, we must view ourselves in the light of Truth.

Truth is the Word of God. Jesus prayed in John 17:17 (NIV), "Sanctify them by the truth; your word is truth." God's Word is life; to go against it will only lead to our spiritual death, which leads to all the natural factors in our life dying until we die physically. To overcome our natural weakness, we must learn to recognize the lies of the enemy and resist the desire to play on emotional trauma. The moment we begin to think like an inferior person, we begin to compromise the life God has already given us. We can't be afraid of the weaknesses or the experiences that led to our phobias or self-deceptions. We must face them with the truth that stands up against any accusation of suggestion.

You don't have to live in a lie. You don't have to live in fear of someone finding out your weaknesses or secret sins. You do not have to live in bondage over what used to be. The enemy would love to keep you trapped in the prison of your mind, never allowing yourself to grow and develop into your God-given purpose. The enemy will play on your natural desires and then use sin to keep you grounded. Well, I got news for you: even if you feel you have committed the worst sin ever, it has not stopped God from loving you. He still has a plan for you amid your weakness. I desire to inspire you and teach you what I am learning each day: to face their fears and overcome every weakness by standing up to them and recognizing the setups of failure as they come.

## Chapter 2

# Don't Hide From Truth

**Genesis 3:7-10 (NIV)**

"Then the eyes of both of them were opened, and they realized they were naked; so, they sewed fig leaves together and made coverings for themselves. Then the man and his wife heard the sound of the LORD God as he was walking in the garden in the cool of the day, and they hid from the LORD God among the trees of the garden. But the LORD God called to the man, "Where are you?" He answered, "I heard you in the garden, and I was afraid because I was naked; so I hid."

I want to begin this chapter by speaking about sin and falling short. All have done it. As the author, I, too, have failed to do everything God has called me to do.

So, don't rush to beat yourself up. The best thing to do is to respond to the call of God.

Unfortunately, running was the response God got from Adam. When Adam and Eve took the forbidden fruit, their eyes opened to sin. They saw flaws in their life, primarily in their nakedness. For the first time, they saw the masterpiece of their body, formed in the image of God for good, as a flawed work. So, they tried to hide the issue behind leaves. Leaning on their understanding—this is what many of us try to do when we have weaknesses in our lives. We try to hide behind things we believe will cover up the real issue. We try to display a life we've made to look good to the world around us. The world sees our job, which appears successful, or our family with a supposedly happy marriage and picture-perfect children. Or they see the trips we take and post on social media that display a life of memories—but these things can never replace the joy of being truly free. We avoid the conversation with a loving God who wants to rectify and fill the void that our sin caused.

This void in the heart can only be filled by the Father's love. God's Word is powerful, and to the person that will believe it, His Word will begin a process of purification. Your life is not beyond the blood of Jesus. God's love for you is powerful. While He does not love sin, He never stops loving you. The actions we commit outside of His love will have consequences, as Adam found out.

> **Genesis 3:17 (KJV)"And unto Adam he said, Because thou hast hearkened unto the voice of thy wife, and hast eaten of the tree, of which I**

**commanded thee, saying, Thou shalt not eat of it: cursed is the ground for thy sake; in sorrow shalt thou eat of it all the days of thy life"**

Please understand that Adam committed a severe transgression of disobedience, and it resulted in the curse plaguing the earth. He lost the authority of God's blessing and committed it to the hands of his new lord, the devil. Because of this transfer of power, sin became the way of life. The absence of God's Spirit of life was the void in the heart of Adam. While he knew of God, he lost the intimate relationship. Their divine communication and fellowship had been severed by disobedience. Sin is a hard taskmaster. It drives us by fear and intimidation, and these thoughts are promoted by the accuser of the brethren—the devil. God did not make you for sin. He did not make hell for you. It was meant for the devil and his angels.

Satan would love to keep you trapped in your past. The enemy's formula for a fallen man or woman begins with a constant connection to past mistakes and failures, areas of abandonment, or mistreatment at the hands of another. If the enemy can keep you constantly reminded of what was, you will always run from God, who is trying to show you what can be. Thoughts that plague the mind are the weapons of the enemy to keep you trapped in brokenness. These thoughts usually manifest in some type of outward action like addictions to drugs, sex or sexual perversion, gambling, lying, and cheating. They can create an attitude of anger and rage, apathy and depression, suicidal thoughts, and murder. These behaviors are the fruit of the curse; they are not and will never be the will of God for your life. Therefore,

God desires to fellowship intimately and personally with you. No matter the experiences and weaknesses we have had, God is asking us to bring it all to Him. He already knows what has taken place and what the root cause is. He is not turned away by our life scars; He is drawn to them. The key to it all is responding to God in truth and transparency. God is a redeemer, and you mean a great deal to Him. He always comes back to us when we fall to past mistakes and failures. It's best to respond to God when we know we have errored or taken a path that we know was not His will for our lives, or the life of disobedience will continue to produce great pressure and aggravation in our lives.

Christ has redeemed us from the curse of the law, having become a curse for us. "For it is written, 'Cursed *is* everyone who hangs on a tree'" Galatians 3:13 [New King James Version (NKJV)]. Sin does not have to rule us. When we begin to understand God's great love through Christ Jesus, we are set free from all past actions, and it liberates us to walk in closer fellowship with a Holy God who only desires to lead us into a life that models His. You are not your last mistake or any other error that has caused you shame.

The battles we face will try to make us walk away from the truth of God's plan through Christ. They come through testing, trials, and temptations. These forces try to keep us thinking through our natural ability, and they try to make us think only within the sphere of our influence. This mindset drives you back to the forbidden fruit, reliving the cycle all over again and layering the shame. If you're like me, you get tired of coming out under the weight of one hurt to another; it requires a determined man or woman who will stand up and say, "Enough is enough." You don't have to live in a cycle of heartbreak. God has an amazing plan for you. Even though Adam sinned and tried to hide it, God clothed Him. Genesis 3:21 (KJV) **"Unto Adam also and to his wife did the LORD God make coats of skin's and clothed them."**

What an awesome example of the loving goodness of God. It represents the life that was to come in His Son, Jesus, who would become the perfect love of God in the flesh and cover all our sins. Blood had to be shed, but instead of killing Adam and Eve, He slaughtered an animal to cover them. He used a substitute.

Our lives operate on the same agenda. Christ in us is the life of God. The Word is the commandment of God. Living on the inside of us is the Holy Spirit, the life counselor, and lead truth instructor. Understand that the issues you face are not the final decision on your destiny. God has a plan for you regardless of what you have been through, what you've done, or what you've experienced. The enemy would have you believe that your mistakes have pushed God away— that the best thing for you to do is to hide your issues. But that couldn't be further from the truth. To defeat the demons of your past and become free from past failures and issues you must face them head-on, and this will require you to look at yourself from a different perspective or through a different lens.

# Chapter 3

# A Better Lens

**Matthew 6:22 NIV**

**"The eye is the lamp of the body. If your eyes are healthy,[a] your whole body will be full of light.**

Religion has become one of the most dangerous forms of the human belief system. The church has, in many minds today, become a formality—an obligatory checklist of things to do—leaving the most influential aspect of the faith, like developing a relationship with God and walking out a spirit-led life through faith in the finished works of Jesus. The numbness of church attendance, hiding the true pains of life. Please know that I do not speak from a platform of condemnation, because I've lived under a false identity of faking my mood and lying about my truest state of affairs. I was making statements about being blessed when people would ask How I was doing when I was hurting inside—pressing the smile on my face when I really wanted to cry for help.

I participated in the service singing on the praise team, teaching the youth, serving the community, and engaging in every church endeavor. I plastered a smile on my face and used the colloquial church phrases. Meanwhile, at home, I was bound to depression and trapped in sexual addiction. Granted, I saw God do amazing things in the life of our youth and others I served. I just couldn't see God moving in my own life. It was as if God was very real for others, but I couldn't realize His life-changing power for myself.

This was a very frustrating time in my life. It was not the ministry's fault. It wasn't God's fault. Church itself was not the means to my pitfalls; my lack of commitment to developing a relationship with God and His Spirit was my issue. I was committed to the form of godliness, but I denied His power to transform my life. God would use the church and His believers as a healing agent in my life.

At that time, I couldn't understand why I did not see the breakthrough in my life. I didn't see myself in the light of God's truth. I had allowed the enemy to convince me that the battle in my mind and the issues that I had were the real defining initiatives of my life. I had perceived that reading the Bible, teaching, and singing were as close to God as I would get. The frustration I felt and the depression that I was in was just a part of being disobedient, and life continued to decline from that moment.

As I reflect, I realize that my perception of God became skewed by the rejection I felt when I was released from the Baltimore Ravens in 2002. Professional sports became my end goal; it was what I had associated myself with and recognized as my purpose in life. Being rejected from the one thing I thought I was skilled in became the lens through which I saw God's thoughts of me. The best I could do was to show up for church and participate in the things I had been taught to do.

All the faith teaching I heard went down the drain, and I was teaching it. It was easy to speak to someone else about living by faith, but I kept my mouth shut when it came to the issues of my life. I began to hide from the real issue when the answer was living on the inside. I used ministries as fig leaves. Yes, you can use ministry as a cover, just as you can with a drug, food, shopping, or any other addiction. I viewed ministry as a so-called "good addiction," but anything that has our focus outside of Christ is bondage—a fig leaf. Our faith in Jesus is the greatest source of freedom. We are, and we see things based on the way we believe. **God is not bound by our issues; He is bound by our unbelief. The sin that places people in bondage is not what you did; it is what you didn't believe.**

> **"See to it, brothers and sisters, that none of you has a sinful, unbelieving heart that turns away from the living God." Hebrews 3:12 NIV**

It is not God's desire for you to live your life, believing that you are inadequate and undeserving of a better life. His love for you is greater than any mistake you could ever make. Believing is the most powerful force that we have as human beings, apart from the words we speak. Believing carries the greatest influence on what we do and whom we become.

**"For as he thinketh in his heart, so is he: Eat and drink, saith he to thee; but his heart is not with thee"** (Proverbs 23:7 KJV).

Notice what the scripture says: as he thinks in his heart, so is he. You are what you think you are. The mind operates on images and visions. Your mind was meant to take the goodness of God and bring forth His good image and demonstrate it in the world. Due to the curse of sin, our imagination has been corrupted. Devices such as the "Tell-a-Vision" and the cell phone have distorted the true reality of life.

We have settled for something far from the life of God. The thoughts and images given through many devices today, bring the wrong message in the light of the Gospel. It will cause us to take on the lens of condemnation; therefore, we view the Word of God incorrectly. God's Word is holy. When we look at purity through the lens of condemnation, the enemy works in our minds bringing about shame, which causes us to hide from the truth. We then don't feel worthy enough to speak or act on what God says. We begin using terms like, "When I fix this, I will come to church," or "I want to straighten out somethings in my life before I give my life to God." Can I tell you the truth? We, in ourselves, will never reach God's mark on our own. Our sins are greater than any of our efforts, so we will never find the right time to come to God, But God is awesome; He took care of the sin issue before we ever committed the act.

"Blessed be the God and Father of our Lord Jesus Christ, who hath blessed us with all spiritual blessings in heavenly places in Christ: **According to as he hath chosen us in him before the foundation of the world,**

*A Better Lens*

**that we should be holy and without blame before him in love" Ephesians 1:3-4 KJV**

God chose you for Himself before the foundation of the world. Take time to consider the magnitude of those words. God chose us knowing what we would do, how far from Him, we would try to run at times, and still predestined a way for us to be acceptable to Him. God chose you, even in the state that you are in right now. This is what you need to believe. This is good news: the Gospel. This is the image we should determine to keep each day. Ephesians goes on to say that we, you and I, should be holy and without blame. God is not blaming you for anything. He has set you free through the work of His Son, Jesus, our substitute for every wrongdoing we have committed or ever will commit. Think a3bout this!

The Apostle John captured this revelation in Christ's conversation with Nicodemus.

> **John 3:16-18 (KJV)**
>
> **For God so loved the world, that he gave his only begotten Son, that whosoever believeth in him should not perish, but have everlasting life. For God sent not his Son into the world to condemn the world; but that the world through him might be saved. He that believeth on him is not condemned: but he that believeth not is condemned already, because he hath not believed in the name of the only begotten Son of God.**

God didn't send Jesus to condemn humanity for their lack of faith, religious activity, or past failures and sins. He came to preach peace with God. He asked all the people to believe what He said. Verse 18 gives the power behind this promise: "**He that believeth on him is not condemned.**" Condemnation is a thing of the past when you decide to believe in Christ. It is available for you right now because God accomplished this before He ever created anything. He already saw Christ complete His perfect work; therefore, God could believe in humankind even before Jesus ever died and rose again. Now that's the faith of God! He asks you to have the same faith in His Word. It is His commitment to you. The remainder of verse 18 says that **"he that believeth not is condemned already, because he hath not believed in the name of the only begotten Son of God."** When we do not receive God's Word (His Son), we condemn ourselves. It's not God who condemns you or me; it's our wrong thinking and believing our wrong vision.

The lens of condemnation will only cause you to run from God's unconditional love into the hand of the enemy, who will rule over you with fear tactics. Condemnation will try to keep you from walking closer to God. It will overwhelm you with the thought that God wants nothing to do with you because you have an addiction, and God is Holy. It will tell you that having a child out of wedlock disqualifies you from God's. This perception will keep you from endeavoring to have a greater commitment to God, simply because you see yourself as unworthy of a Holy God's attention. But beloved reader, God's love doesn't ever make you feel ashamed or fearful.1 John 4:18 (NKJV) **"There is no fear in love; but perfect love casts out fear, because**

**fear involves torment. But he who fears has not been made perfect in love."**

Fear torments you. Webster's Dictionary (1828) defines *torment* as extreme pain or anguish of body or mind. A mind tormented is a mind that carries mental visions of suffering and pain. Thoughts deceive us into believing that we deserve every bad thing that happens because of what we did, or that worse is coming because we failed to keep a commitment to stop drinking and, in a moment of weakness, found ourselves in the bottle again. The condemnation will torment you until you give up and see yourself as an alcoholic. This form of thinking drives the life of sin and death—thoughts that tell you that you will never succeed or that someone else is better than you because their life appears to be on another level.

The enemy uses our weaknesses to keep us bound to our past and engrossed in the sensual world around us. These erroneous images do not come from God. God is love, as the scripture says in I John 4:8. Therefore, there can't be any fear in His vision for you. You are not your mistakes or past sins. When you realize the gift that God has given you and the life He has given you despite all your sins, boldness will rise in you, and you will look right at the issues in your life and say I am not afraid anymore. This is the victory that comes by faith. It's time to begin to see your life the right way. See yourself the way God sees you.

## Chapter 4

# New Image

**2 Corinthians 5:17** (NIV)[17]

**Therefore, if anyone is in Christ, the new creation has come:**[a] **The old has gone, the new is here!**

Picture this scene: You wake up one morning to the sun peeping through your window. As your eyes open, you hear your alarm clock. It's Monday morning, work is waiting, and the weekend didn't yield much time for rest, so you're still tired. Reluctantly you get out of the bed. In your mind, you know you aren't prepared for work. Most of the people in your department get on your nerves. You recall the weekend. You had both productive and unproductive moments, and you try to understand how you wasted so much time. As you walk towards the bathroom to brush your teeth and wash your face, you glance into the mirror. What do you see?

As I have already stated, what you believe is who you will become. For many, the thoughts that plague our minds place us in a very inferior position. The image we see is not favorable; if it were, the smile on our faces would beam in the mirror. And regardless of how the morning began, we would quickly shake ourselves free from the negative thoughts and revive our attitude. When we look in the mirror, we see what we believe we are.

God's image must become the determiner of our ideal vision for ourselves. Your outward appearance pales in comparison to the person whom God has placed on the inside. Every sin committed was in the flesh. The enemy and his dark forces will make every effort to keep you thinking by your flesh or feelings. These feelings don't indicate the true nature of your new identity in Christ.

**"Ephesians 4:17-24 (NLT)**

**With the Lord's authority I say this: Live no longer as the Gentiles do, for they are hopelessly confused. Their minds are full of darkness; they wander far from the life God gives because they have closed their minds and hardened their hearts against him. They have no sense of shame. They live for lustful pleasure and eagerly practice every kind of impurity. But that isn't what you learned about Christ. Since you have heard about Jesus and have learned the truth that comes from him, throw off your old sinful nature and**

**your former way of life, which is corrupted by lust and deception. Instead, let the Spirit renew your thoughts and attitudes. Put on your new nature, created to be like God—truly righteous and holy."**

The old life is over; you are redeemed. I know it can be hard to discern sometimes given the nature of your current circumstances, but you have. Mind renewal is a process. Faith and the revelation of God's grace is a journey. It requires a strong mind committed to believing God and to walking away daily from the person you used to be. To get rid of the older person, you must be willing to confront them. As this scripture states, throw off the old sinful nature and your old former life. It goes on to instruct you to put on your new nature or character. This nature is said to be righteous and holy! When you came to Christ, you received, and you took on His character. This image becomes evident, the more you submit yourself to the Word of God.

Verse 23 says, "**Instead, let the Spirit renew your thoughts and attitudes.**" The Spirit of God is now alive in you. It is this Spirit in you that helps you begin to see yourself as God has called you. The person you see in the bathroom mirror is true to the natural, but it is not the truth of the Spirit, and God is Spirit. He gives us His Word to deliver us from ourselves (Psalms 107:20). His Word becomes your new mirror.

**"James 1:22-26 (NKJV)**

**But be doers of the word, and not hearers only, deceiving yourselves. For**

> **if anyone is a hearer of the word and not a doer, he is like a man observing his natural face in a mirror; for he observes himself, goes away, and immediately forgets what kind of man he was. But he who looks into the perfect law of liberty and continues *in it and* is not a forgetful hearer but a doer of the work, this one will be blessed in what he does."**

Notice that James, half-brother of Jesus, speaks of the Word as a mirror; the Word is our first viewpoint of the person that we have been called to be. It doesn't reflect what you have done; it reflects who God is in you. It reveals the true nature of the Son that God birthed on the inside of you. The enemy does not want you to see this most vital part of you—the reality that has no flaws or issues, the part of you that is blessed with all the heavenly blessings (Ephesians 1:3). We are told to be a doer of the Word, to make our spiritual nature a reality.

He goes on to say that when we read the commandments of the Word and then live differently, it's like looking into a mirror and seeing yourself one way and then going and behaving another. For example, imagine someone left you an inheritance. It's written on a document. The lawyer helps you discern what has rightfully been given to you. He reads all the terms and conditions to you, and what has been left to you makes you a billionaire. In a second, you have gone from rags to riches. Everything you need is now within your grasp; you want for nothing. You can help all the people that you desire to help and start the company you so long to start. But shortly after the meeting you walk out to your car and forget what you have. You see a person in need and want to do something about it. You dream about the business that would employ so many but become discouraged because you don't believe you have the resources to accomplish it. I know that sounds crazy, but this is how many believers live.

We see the wrong image. We live with a "lack of" mentality rather than a plentiful mindset. You have been liberated and set free from your past. God never told you to be perfect to serve Him. He told you to believe what He said and act accordingly.

What keeps you from becoming what you've dreamed about being? Usually, it is a wrong self-image. That addiction is not who you are. You are not the sexual perversion that has plagued you for years. The divorce doesn't define you; neither does any neglect, molestation, or abuse. Christ has redeemed you from your past. Through the Word of God, you can overcome the toil and daily aggravation of life's traumatic experiences. We are to take on a new image, and that nature is the image of the perfect Son of God. Understand you have the authority to put the devil and his opinions under your feet. You will see yourself as a champion, as an overcomer. You are the righteousness of God in Christ. Keep this on your mind and speak it continually from your mouth. You will take your life back!

## Chapter 5

# Shut Up, Snake

**James 4:7 (NIV)**

**⁷Submit yourselves, then, to God. Resist the devil, and he will flee from you.**

*Accuser*: to charge with a fault or offense: blame. (Webster 1828) The devil is known as the accuser of the brethren. **Revelation 12:10 (NKJV) "Then I heard a loud voice saying in heaven, 'Now salvation, and strength, and the Kingdom of our God, and the power of His Christ have come, for the accuser of our brethren, who accused them before our God day and night, has been cast down.'**

The enemy would love to keep you stuck in the past. Sin is a horrible slave master, driven by the power of fear. But thanks be to God we have been saved from the power of sin. For this purpose, we must keep the mind renewed because the temptation of the enemy does not come blatantly. It always comes as subtle suggestions that feed a hidden desire that already existed in our flesh. These thoughts are meant to keep us in a cycle of recurring bad habits. Remember how he tempted Adam and Eve and remember the way the Bible spoke to the serpent's cunning and crafty ways. His gestures lead Adam and Eve into spiritual death and inevitably natural death.

The whole deal could have been shut down if the man of God had stood up and told the serpent where to go. The authority was the man's; it didn't belong to the serpent. I believe that Adam could have redeemed Eve, being that he was a type and shadow of Jesus who was to come and redeem us all. Adam had the power to shut the whole thing down by speaking from his place of authority. We have the same right in Christ to speak to the situations in our lives. Sometimes you must tell the darkness in your mind, "Shut Up!" Your mind and emotions were not meant to be dominated by the threats and fears of the past life.

The trauma of not reaching my end goal of becoming a professional athlete and the constant thought of not being enough resounded in my mind all the time. No matter how many positive things I had in my life, the thought remained: I failed. The authority to overcome this mindset was in me, sports didn't define me, but I became a slave to the idea. Those thoughts would be tied to other thoughts of my childhood. Times, when promises were broken by my parents or things, didn't work out the way I planned. These accusations of the enemy were his tactics to keep me at a low level of thinking. Failure will never be God's thoughts about you. One moment doesn't stop God's eternal plan.

Thoughts of defeat, shame, and failure are meant to make you feel as if you haven't already received all that you need in Christ. The Bible speaks about Satan as the adversary. The word adversary means one that contends with, opposes, or resists: an enemy or opponent.

> **"1 Peter 5:8-10 (NKJV)**
>
> **Be sober, be vigilant; because your adversary the devil walks about like a roaring lion, seeking whom he may devour. Resist him, steadfast in the faith, knowing that the same sufferings are experienced by your brotherhood in the world. But may the God of all grace, who called us to His eternal glory by Christ Jesus, after you have suffered a while, perfect, establish, strengthen, and settle *you*."**

I want to break this verse down and explore the riches in this exert from Peter's letter. He tells the reader to be sober and vigilant. This is a state of mind, and the mind is fixed on the Light of Truth. The Truth is God's Word. So, he's telling us to know the Truth of God's Word and keep it on our minds, because the devil tries to walk like a lion. He is not a lion by any means, but he wants to present himself as a big threat. His threat is opposition to your position in Christ. He wants to use his words to create images in your mind that provoke fear, and like a flock of wildebeest, we run frantically, separating ourselves from the safety of wise counsel, or like a flock of sheep we run from our Shepard. It is in those isolated, fearful moments that he has been given the right to take over your mind. Lives are destroyed because we allow our minds to run rampant with negative thoughts about ourselves.

Notice the scripture says that the enemy is seeking whom he *may* destroy, not who he *will* destroy. This emphasizes the object of his seeking: us. He seeks to find weak-minded individuals that will fall for the trap. Please do not take this offensively; I, too, have fallen into this state of mind and the emotional trap of offense, strife, gossip, and slander and the images of shame, defeat, failure, and unworthiness.

These thoughts don't come from God; they come from the adversary, the devil. Don't give in to the lie. Resist him. And how do you do that? By drawing closer to God through His Word. James 4:7 NIV says, "**Submit yourselves, then, to God. Resist the devil, and he will flee from you.**." The power of resistance is in drawing closer to God in your relationship with Him. The power comes from knowing Him. The enemy can't defeat God, and he knows it. Can I take it a step further? The enemy can't defeat you, but he is counting on the fact that you don't know it. Therefore, he seeks a weak vessel to destroy. Resistance is an enduring process because the battlefield of the mind is an ongoing, 24/7 process. Thoughts, words, and images cross our minds at a rapid rate. The key to winning the war is in your mouth. **Proverbs 18:21 (KJV) "Death and life are in the power of the tongue: and they that love it shall eat the fruit thereof."**

God has given us power and a choice to say whatever we want. But there is more to speaking than just saying words. There is power, miraculous power, in the things you say. You may not always see it, but there is a cause and effect to each word we decree from our lips. Words have the power to declare our position. Jesus said, "For by your words you will be acquitted, and by your words, you will be condemned."(Matthew 12:37

*Shut Up, Snake*

NIV). This scripture references the importance of what you say about yourself or your situation. How you communicate determines where you end up.

I heard it said that the only person you're going to believe all the time is yourself. Therefore, choose your words mindfully. In my fight, I had to cling to and truly believe the Word of God for myself, not simply to teach others. I began to realize the living power of what God's Word can do. Things hidden in me began to become clear. Issues that I had not dealt with began to manifest—not in a condemning way, but from an authoritative position that spoke truth to the matter. The little boy in me was crying out for healing inside of a grown man. My breakthrough came through speaking to myself. I had to resist the urge to give in to past hurts and disappointments. The accusations of my past were not going to be the final verdict of my future. I began to testify as a witness for myself through the life of Christ and say my life is just like His life.

The thoughts didn't go away immediately, but their hold began to weaken the more I committed to speaking God's Word and truth over my life. My image of myself changed as I saw my life fulfilled. I began to tell my snake to "Shut up!"

Thoughts of the past want to creep back into your thinking. Open your mouth and communicate the Word of God. I am the righteousness of God in Christ. I am a new man or woman in Christ Jesus. My old self passed away, and I am new.

> Tell that lying snake to shut up. The enemy loves to operate in the dark; he is stealthy in his approach. Darkness can only be dispelled by one force: LIGHT!

> The Word of God is light! God and His Word must become your defense against the words and images trying to plague your mind. **Your word is a lamp for my feet, a light on my path.** Psalms 119:105 NIV

A dark room is an uncertain place for a person that had never been in the room before the lights went out. The uncertainty can be scary when trying to navigate through the room because you don't know what's there. But when the lights are on, the darkness is dispelled, and you can see where you are going without stumbling.

**Proverbs 6:23 (NKJV)**

> "For the commandment *is* a lamp, And the law a light; Reproofs of instruction *are* the way of life"

God's Word in our lives is the anchor that sustains us and keeps us on the path of life, and not just any life but the life that He designed. This is beyond our human comprehension and can only be revealed through a Spirit that is just like His. And that Spirit comes alive the day you make Jesus Christ your Lord. I must go deeper into this to strengthen your faith in the power of your words to defeat the thoughts in your mind. God gave you an amazing gift, and we are going to bring clarity to HIM alive in you.

## Chapter 6

# Wake Up

**Ephesians 5:14 (NKJV)**

**"Therefore, He says: 'Awake, you who sleep, Arise from the dead, And Christ will give you light.'"**

Amazing work is taking place on the inside of you as a believer in the Lord Jesus Christ. What God has done is truly a miracle. God in His triune being has come alive inside you by the Holy Spirit. The person of Christ lives inside of you right now as a believer. God wants us to wake up and realize the true nature of our inward self and stop sleeping on the gift we have on the inside.

God is light, and in Him, there is no darkness (I John 1:5). On the day of your salvation, God came alive in you. His Light lit up your human Spirit, and you became a son of God. Born again into His family. The faith that Jesus had in the earth became the faith that you received on the inside. The grace of the Holy Spirit became the grace that empowers you to live above sin. **Proverbs 20:27 (KJV) "The spirit of man is the candle of the LORD, searching all the inward parts of the belly."**

If you have made Christ Lord of your life, then God has His life alive in you and that life desires to come alive. It desires to reveal the true nature of your life. Nothing in your past can change what God has just done on the inside of you. You have become a perfect being inwardly. I know that word *perfect* can be scary. The reason is that we have been taught to see perfection through the eyes of our efforts. The issue is that everything we have done to this point has been nowhere close to perfection; this is where the Spirit of God differentiates us from our old conscience.

The Spirit that God gives is Holy. This Spirit is filled with love, joy, righteousness, peace, self-control, and humility. We've heard about these attributes but have found them very hard to live by. But God, through Jesus Christ, has given us the Spirit to assist us in becoming this type of person. Right now, you are right with God; you are in perfect standing, full of love in the eyes of God. You are without blame. Isn't that awesome and liberating?

The thoughts in your mind about not being enough or meeting a standard can be destroyed right now by simply taking God at His Word. God's Word is powerful enough to take you from one level of life into another. His Spirit will teach you how to become the person He has called you to be all along.

The best way to deal with a problem is head-on, but it's always difficult to address something that you don't feel you are qualified or capable of dealing with. Fear desires to keep you in darkness, stumbling over past mistakes, and trapped in the thoughts of failure. These lies cause us to remain stagnant and immobile. We refuse to change and become bitter and develop strife with anyone that challenges us to change. This heart and mindset didn't come from God.

No matter how much you know or how much you have grown, we will always be in an ever-growing process of learning. God is so vast and His knowledge so great that we can spend one thousand lifetimes searching it and still never fully achieve it. The Gospel of Jesus Christ is rich with the newness of life and freedom, but it comes through the revelation of God's amazing love and the gift of His Holy Spirit. We must become acquainted with perfect, unconditional love, and the gift of empowering grace. God is not afraid of your past; He is not afraid of your sins. This is why He sent Jesus to prove to us that there is a power in man that can destroy sin and win over it every time.

Jesus came as the Light to expose the lie of the devil and then later strip it of its power. Jesus is our example. Looking at Him should teach us and remind us that nothing we have done or are currently going through has a say in our future. Life has a way of presenting many things to us, and for many people, we receive these circumstances as our lot in life. We take them as a part of life. I think of it as a housemate. We allow negative thoughts to live in our minds, and we communicate the problems like they are a permanent tenant. These things do not have a right to torment you—or live in your life. 1 John 4:18 (NIV) **"There is no fear in love. But perfect love drives out fear, because fear has to do with punishment. The one who fears is not made perfect in love."**

*The Transparent Life & Your Eternal Destiny*

    God has perfect love for you. Not only does He love you perfectly, but He has also given you perfect love in your heart (Romans 5:5). This revelation should not only tell you how great God's love is but, the more you meditate on it; it should become very real to your heart. This revelation will empower you to see yourself in a different light. You are not far from God or His salvation. This person is alive inside of you right now. You can look right at all your mistakes and past failures and say, "I am a new person in Christ Jesus." You don't have to answer to the past anymore. The Light has a way of exposing areas of darkness in our lives; this isn't something you should fear. Remember, God knew you had the issues before you did, and He made way for you to bring those issues to Him. He loves you so much that He wants to work with you no matter what condition you are in. He started the work. He will complete it if given the time and your heart.

*Chapter 7*

## See HIM!

**Colossians 1:27 (KJV)**

**"To whom God would make known what is the riches of the glory of this mystery among the Gentiles; which is Christ in you, the hope of glory"**

The life of God in you is called His glory. Glory is Light, revealed knowledge, weighty presence; it is a spiritual reality. Everything we need is in the spirit. God wants to reveal life to you by watching Christ. His life will give understanding to your spirit and unlock truths that will help you overcome and succeed in life. **Hebrews 4:14-16 (NIV) "Therefore, since we have a great high priest who has ascended into heaven, Jesus the Son of God, let us hold firmly to the faith we profess. For we do not have a high priest who is unable to empathize with our weaknesses, but we have one who has been tempted in every way, just as we are—yet he did not sin."**

Jesus suffered through temptations as well. He was tempted but never sinned, and this speaks volumes to us today. Now before you jump to conclusions and say, "Well, He was Jesus; He was divinity," let me remind you that He stripped Himself of His divinity to wear humanity. He was born of the Spirit but still had to be baptized, and it wasn't until He had withstood the temptation of the devil that He would walk in the power of the Spirit. He is our example. We have received the power of the spirit through the new birth. Therefore, the power to live like Christ has been imparted to us through the gracious gift of the Holy Spirit.

Now, Jesus had opportunities to give in to His flesh: to say things that the Father did not tell Him to say; to do things the Father did not reveal to Him; to treat people disrespectfully and apathetically. But this is not the way He did ministry. He had to deal with demons—both around Him and those who spoke to Him directly. Yet Jesus never coward down nor fell to the thoughts and words of the enemy. He dealt with them directly because He understood His authority. Mark 1:32-34 (NIV) **"That evening after sunset the people brought to Jesus all the sick and demon-possessed. The whole town gathered at the door, and Jesus healed many who had various diseases. He also drove out many demons, but he would not let the demons speak because they knew who he was."**

Jesus knew who He was! Do you know who you are? He didn't deal with darkness from a position of being lower than them but from a position of knowing that they were subject to Him. Those who were tormented by the demons were saved because Jesus told the demonic forces what to do. He didn't even allow them to weigh in on the matter. This wasn't always the case, as we will see a little later in this chapter, but in this case, He didn't have a conversation or debate with the issue.

What is it that you are facing? In Christ, you have been given the power and authority to begin to address that issue with the words of your mouth and with the corresponding action. God has given all of us through Christ Jesus a life free from the bondage of past mistakes and the fear of future problems. Nothing that happens in our lives has the power to separate us from what God has done through Jesus Christ. God has purposed you for good. Your life was meant to produce good things. The enemy would love nothing more than to get you caught up in shame and condemnation because that takes your eyes off the goal and the vision of life that God has purposed you for. Jesus is the answer to our shortcomings. No matter how bad we think our mistakes are or how great our past, Christ is greater.

Colossians 3:3 (KJV)

**"For ye are dead, and your life is hid with Christ in God."**

Notice the scripture referenced here. It says that we are dead, and our life is hidden in Christ. This death mentioned is not a physical one, which is obvious because you are reading this book. That means this death is speaking to something else. This death speaks to who you were before you came back to the knowledge of God for your life. You may have faced some very serious situations before you heard the gospel, but the day you believed what Jesus did for you on the cross, you died. The past of who you used to be is no longer your reality. In the mind of God, you are righteous and blameless in His sight. Why? Because the Spirit of Christ has come alive in you. Your life is now hidden in a new spiritual nature.

*You must see yourself in Christ. God doesn't see you as you see yourself. He sees you as He sees Christ, the perfect Son. Jesus obeyed the Father perfectly. The Father is pleased with Jesus. Can I reveal something to you? The Father is pleased with you. In Christ, you have been given the same outcome as Jesus. Therefore, the Word of God is paramount in your study and meditation. Becoming one with the Word of God will help you see the life of Christ more clearly. You must see Christ and allow the Holy Spirit to reveal Him more clearly to you.*

*This is a process; it doesn't happen overnight. Christ in you will be revealed at the level in which you seek Him out. Matthew 7:7-8 (NIV) says, "Ask, and it will be given to you; seek, and you will find; knock, and the door will be opened to you. For everyone who asks receives; the one who seeks finds; and to the one who knocks, the door will be opened." Jeremiah 29:13 (NIV) says, "You will seek me and find me when you seek me with all your heart." God doesn't want to be the mystery; many would say He does. He is a liberal giver. It is His good pleasure to give us the Kingdom. See Luke 12:32. He desires you to see His redemptive power and plan for your life hidden in Christ.*

*I have spent many days looking at my own life through the lens of my failures. Fear is a wicked and crippling taskmaster. You will always hide from the giants of shame and rejection when you are afraid of the threat that comes with past hurts. It will make you feel small and inadequate. These feelings are not in Christ. These are the things He bore in His body for you. When we begin to see Him more than we see ourselves, we are empowered to face the challenges face to face. We can stand up to the addiction or sexual perversion, failing marriage, or financial problem.*

*To beat your foe, you must have authority and power greater than your oppressor. Christ wants to be formed in you. T*his is not something you feel all the time; it is something you receive by faith in God's Word. In other words, whatever God says about you is the Truth. Believing what He spoke in His Word is the reality of the person you are on the inside. What you see, hear, and feel around you will contradict this reality, but you can't let that disrupt your connection to the Truth of what God said. God's Word is more powerful than our issues, and it doesn't stop being true because we have setbacks or problems. It was spoken before any of this ever happened, knowing we would have these moments in life.

Therefore, you have no reason to hide from God. He has redeemed you. Your best life is not in what you can do for yourself, but it is in having faith in what Jesus has done for you. You must begin to look at Him more than you look at yourself. Deliverance many times comes through the process, and that process is a matter of perception or belief. We become what we place our belief in. Christ is the perfect man of God. He obeyed the Father perfectly; He is the perfect Son. In Him and in the Spirit, we become the perfect Son in the eyes of God. We now have a process of matriculation into the image of the Son of God. We cannot do this in our strength; we need help, and God graces us with giftings that will assist us in becoming all that He predestined us to be.

If we look solely on ourselves, we see nothing that would please God. In ourselves, we come short in many of the things that a Holy God requires. We see our debt, our addictions, our brokenness, and our confusion. We see the marriage that didn't work out and the broken promises committed against us—the list goes on and on. These thoughts cause us to hide who we are many times. But I assure you, God is not bothered by who we used to be or the history that burdens us in the present moment. It is not for us to hide, but to reveal as we are hidden in Christ. Beloved—and that's who YOU ARE, His beloved—you are so free in this moment even though you feel captive. I am asking you at this moment to place more trust in God than you do your experiences and start searching for Christ. God is not a man; His promises last eternally.

*Chapter 8*

# God Is Not a Man

**Numbers 23:19 (NIV)**

**"God is not human, that he should lie, not a human being, that he should change his mind. Does he speak and then not act? Does he promise and not fulfill?"**

Those Words should go without the need for expository, but they do. Why? Because in our finite thinking, we all come to places in our life where we begin to think that God's ability to save us and preserve us is based on some human characteristic or attribute. As I consider my own life, I look at some of the decisions I have made and see the places where I blatantly spoke the truth of God's Word: went to church services and received a very relevant and anointed Word, sung some powerful praise and worship songs with tears and altar worship, then went home and placed my life back into my own hands by allowing life's pressures to deceive me into thinking God couldn't handle it. As I have grown in the Word—and I am still learning, by the way—I have come to recognize in my limited capacity that every time I backslid on the Word of God, it was because somewhere in me, I began to believe God as I did my natural father.

I say that not to belittle my earthly father, but, in our humanity, all of us have come short on promises made. Even with my children, I have made promises, unfortunately, that I didn't follow through on. These experiences cause us to have a mental outlook of failure and insecurity when it comes to promises made. It taints our view of integrity and high character. We accept the apologies of the offender, but inwardly we hold onto the memory of the promise made and broken. Every promise to follow is measured up to the last one, and then those missed opportunities are ranked and weighed on a level of importance. Over time we seemingly forget some of them until a situation happens that reminds us of the moment the infraction occurred. This cycle of highs and lows with no resolution becomes the basis of what we call "trust issues."

Trust is something that is earned, not given. A person that has been hurt frequently by one broken promise after another is prone to become numb to promises and become self-reliant.

When we come to Christ, it becomes our responsibility to learn how to trust God. We must come to understand that God is not human. He is a Spirit. **John 4:24 (NIV) "God is spirit, and his worshipers must worship in the Spirit and in truth."**

Spirits are eternal beings, and the nature and character of the Spirit are eternal. God doesn't change; He is constant. **"Jesus Christ is the same yesterday and**

**today and forever"** (Hebrews 13:8, NIV). These words are profound, and they speak to the nature and integrity of God. We must keep these Words in our eyes and ears so that they become a part of our everyday life. He desires to show us His unconditional love—a love that heals us and causes us to change the way we think, or repent.

Before I received the love of God, I struggled with releasing the issues of my life totally into His care, allowing Him to teach me how to respond and what to do. My heart was hard. Even though I was raised in the church, I had not fully received the Word of God for me. I didn't make anything I read personal. I saw God as this amazing Spirit that could do whatever He wanted. He had all power. I heard that He was my Father and that He loved me. But my human experience made me doubt it. My earthly father and mother did the best they could to provide for my siblings and me, but we didn't always get the things we needed, many times because the finances were not available to purchase the items. Therefore, when I heard that God owned the cattle on a thousand hills, I thought that was cool, but I discounted myself from the qualified recipients of such a promise—as if God was limited to only provide for special people who had a great relationship with Him and walked perfectly; as if He only worked with those of great faith.

Friend, God is not a man; He is not prone to human tendencies. He is a sure thing. Everything He said He would do, He will do and more. He requires one thing from us—FAITH! We must believe that God is a rewarder. He has a desire to meet every need that we have in our lives to the point we overflow into the lives of others and prove God's ability to provide.

If you are suffering today with insecurity and a lack of trust, today is a moment to begin to yield yourself to God. Don't hide the issue; God already knows. It's open before Him. Speak openly to Him and use the Word that you have received in this chapter to give foundation to your prayers. The Bible says in Isaiah 43:26 NIV, **"Put Me in remembrance; Let us contend together; State your *case,* that you may be [a]acquitted.** You are not responsible for proving your qualifications when it comes to God. He holds Himself responsible for His Word. His Word is His justification. God and His Word are one.

**John 1:1 NKJV says**, "**In the beginning was the Word, and the Word was with God, and the Word was God."** Nothing God says is void of His eternal presence. Therefore, when He speaks a promise, it will not come back without accomplishing the task that He spoke it to become. Every Word carries His eternal Spirit. This is the same spirit that Genesis speaks of in the very beginning of creation. Take time to read Genesis 1:1-4.

I desire to compel you to believe every Word from God. It speaks to His character. Isaiah 55:11 says, **"So shall My word be that goes forth from My mouth; It shall not return to Me [a]void, But it shall accomplish what I please, And it shall prosper *in the thing* for which I sent it.** So, what did God send His Word to do? **"He sent His word and healed them, And delivered *them* from their destructions."** (Psalm 107:20). God's Word is the promise of His intentions for your life. Whatever any person has done, forgive them and let it go. God desires to earn your trust. It is His goodness that will cause you to change your mind about Him (Romans 2:4). God has a perspective. He sees you a certain way, and the best thing for you to do is to begin to receive God's opinion over your feelings. He sees beyond the present moment, and He desires to take you into the life He sees. So, what does God see?

*Chapter 9*

# I See YOU!

**Jeremiah 1:5 (NLT)**

**"I knew you before I formed you in your mother's womb. Before you were born, I set you apart and appointed you as my prophet to the nations."**

The beauty of God's presence is in the dialogue between God and His man. In this passage, God is coming to a young man named Jeremiah because He has an assignment for him. It's an assignment to the nation and its leaders, both politically and spiritually. The scripture begins the dialogue with God speaking to Jeremiah and letting him know that, in simple terms, "I know you. I knew you before this world ever received you into it." When God says I knew you, it means to recognize, admit, acknowledge, confess, or to consider; it also means to know, be acquainted with.

God was letting Jeremiah know that the life he was living was not the life God purposed him for. "I know who you are." Life in this world has a way of tainting the true image of God's purpose in our lives. Different situations and setbacks can keep you misinformed of God's true purpose for your life. God knows who we are, even when we claim to be something else. Jeremiah, like many of us, didn't believe that he was qualified to pick up the mantle that God was calling Him to. God told him, "I appointed you before time began." In truth, Jeremiah was meant to be born at the time he was because the nation of Israel needed to repent and return to God. A huge assignment, but he wouldn't do it alone. God was going to be with him. The only prerequisite to this assignment was to agree with God.

God knows us better than we know ourselves. He has an appointment for all our lives. We can't allow our view of ourselves to disrupt God's original view of us. The best thing to do is to follow Him. Jeremiah speaks back to God in this dialogue in Jeremiah 1:6-10 (NLT):

**"' O Sovereign LORD,' I said, 'I can't speak for you! I'm too young!' ⁷ The LORD replied, 'Don't say, "I'm too young," for you must go wherever I send you and say whatever I tell you. And don't be afraid of the people, for I will be with you and will protect you. I, the LORD, have spoken!' Then the LORD reached out and touched my mouth and said, 'Look, I have put my words in your mouth! Today I appoint you to stand up against nations and kingdoms. Some you must uproot and tear down, destroy and overthrow. Others you must build up and plant.'"**

## What Did You Say?

Once again, I want to repeat that God knows the truth about you. Jeremiah wanted to use his youth as a hindrance to the calling of God. He told God, "I am too young." But God told Him, "Don't say, 'I'm too young,' for you must go wherever I send you and say whatever I tell you." The key to the right perspective begins with the words of your mouth. How do you talk about yourself? When you are asked about yourself, how do you respond? Understand responding favorably and in faith doesn't mean everything in your life is perfect in the natural. It means you have decided to believe God over your circumstances. God told him, "Don't tell me what you think about yourself. I have something for you to do, and you can't do it talking like that." Your voice and words go beyond the moment; they speak to your future. They speak to your harvest, purpose, destiny, and legacy.

God's power is in His Word. He doesn't say anything unintentionally; it carries purpose and life-giving power. Therefore, His correction of Jeremiah was not to discourage him but to set the record straight that they were in partnership, and God needed him to begin to look at himself the way He sees Jeremiah. When you speak about yourself, speak from God's perspective, not the past failures or lack of credentials. When God has called you, the Spirit has just become your credentials; His wisdom has become your counsel and speaking platform. It is no longer you who are responsible for the outcome. God places Himself in the position of fulfillment. He is the power behind each word you speak. He will accomplish that which was spoken in faith.

To see yourself correctly, you must attain a new vocabulary. This comes by the hearing of faith, and Ensure capitalization consistency comes by hearing the Word of God. Don't say what you see naturally. Say what God said about you. "I am healed. I am wise. I am redeemed. My past is dead; my future is bright and alive. I am a leader. I am a great husband or wife. I am a great pastor or lay minister." God will work with your mouth if you set it to speak His will.

## Don't Look for Peoples Appreciation

Everyone is not going to like your transformation. The way you communicate is not going to line up with the life people have seen you live up to this point. They only have the past to construct your identity. God told Jeremiah, "**And don't be afraid of the people, for I will be with you and will protect you. I, the Lord, have spoken!**" One of the setbacks of transformation is the desire to belong, the natural desire to be accepted and appreciated, and this type of mentality, while it is genuine and placed in us by God, can be perverted and twisted into doing anything to keep the company.

Some of the company we keep are not in our lives to help promote positive change. Jeremiah was about to speak some strong truth to his nation and its political and spiritual leaders; this was not going to be an easy task. A young man would be rebuking older rulers and those who taught him and watched him grow up. You and I know that such a job will have people looking at you with a certain level of wonder and disgust. Who was to say what they would do once he had spoken all the Word of the Lord, words that would call the nation a harlot, words of judgment for their unfaithfulness to God. This was a tall task.

Our transformation is a tall task. Leaving what we once knew will challenge current relationships. We may have to challenge things that used to be common, traditions that were once a way of living. The enemy will use these thoughts to keep you stuck right where you are. But I rebuke that thought in the Name of Jesus! God told Jeremiah, "Don't be afraid of the people, **for I will be with you and will protect you. I, the LORD, have spoken!"** Your new journey is not alone. God would not call you and save you to leave you to the elements of this world. He is about to make a great example of you for His glory. What people may have thought was impossible is about to become a reality.

Our submission to God's purpose puts God in a position of fulfilling every promise He has made to us. When God begins to do something to your attitude, some acquaintances will not like it. When loving others becomes your normal behavior, some will consider that weird. When your communication begins to change, those friends and family may tell you that you're fake or not acting like yourself. Don't let those words of persecution and accusations stop you from walking with God. You are on the path to transformation and greatness on a level that God has set. Understand that not everyone in your current circle is going to applaud your change, but thank God that there will be others that have been raised to support and nurture your growth. Stay on the path of transformation.

## Chapter 10

# Yes, I AM Weak

**2 Corinthians 12:6-10 (KJV)**

For though I would desire to glory, I shall not be a fool; for I will say the truth: but now I forbear, lest any man should think of me above that which he seeth me to be, or that he heareth of me. And lest I should be exalted above measure through the abundance of the revelations, there was given to me a thorn in the flesh, the messenger of Satan to buffet me, lest I should be exalted above measure. For this thing I besought the Lord thrice, that it might depart from me. And he said unto me, My grace is sufficient for thee: for my strength is made perfect in weakness. Most gladly therefore will I rather glory in my infirmities, that the power of Christ may rest upon me.

> **Therefore I take pleasure in infirmities, in reproaches, in necessities, in persecutions, in distresses for Christ's sake: for when I am weak, then am I strong.**

One of the toughest things to overcome today is a spirit of pride. No one wants to admit that they don't know or that they are afraid or weak. Paul, the Apostle, offers an example of a problem in his life. He is responsible for two-thirds of the New Testament, more than any of the apostles that walked with Jesus. His insight into the work of grace has far outlived him. This revelation was on a spiritual level; He was receiving directly from the Spirit of Christ. He was stoned and left for dead and came back to life. He was shipwrecked during a storm and bitten by a viper and simply shook it off without concern. Yet here we see him appealing to God concerning a messenger that had been opposing him and his ministry—a menace to him and a contradictor to the message of the cross and the finished works of Jesus. He was a true pain to Paul, to the point that he became a major distraction. He was sent to take Paul's eyes off the work that God had him on the insight he was receiving from God to teach the churches.

This was an issue in Paul's life. It was designed to stunt Paul's growth in grace. Just because we have come to Christ doesn't mean that we are immune to problems. The question is, who do you go to when issues arise? Paul went to God, and we see this awesome witness of God's character. Paul asks God to do something about the messenger that was sent to shut him down. Notice God never says no. His answer was the truth: My grace is the answer.

*Yes, I Am Weak*

The truth is that we are all weak without God. We have no strength in the flesh. We know nothing within ourselves. God is Jehovah Jireh; He is a provider. He desires to be the one who meets our needs. You are in a covenant relationship with Almighty God. Covenant relationships are built on the status of strengths. In a covenant between two people, both have strengths, and the strengths of each individual are meant to cover the weakness of the other by making up what is lacking. This creates an environment of confidence to do the impossible. You spend more time thinking and doing what you're good at rather than being bogged down by trying to figure out how to do what you're not strong at. Your partner picks up the weight on that issue, and you, in return, assist your partner in doing the things they are not good at because it is an area in which you excel.

I am not a plumber. For that matter, when it comes to handiwork, I am not the most proficient, and my wife knows it. When things need to be fixed in our house, like a water heater that needs to be replaced, we have a problem. For me to try and do that job would be very tedious and toilsome because I haven't committed myself to the training and certification that is needed. Attempting it on my own may appear to save money because I don't have to pay the labor cost, but it can end up costing me more when I find out I have left out key components during installation. Then I'd have to call a professional to complete the job, someone with the ability to diagnose the problem and provide the solution accurately while I get back to the things I know I have been called to do. I can confidently say this because I have made many mistakes trying to fix things in my home just to save a dollar here and there. When things break around my house, it is good to have partnerships or a covenant with people that excel where I am not proficient.

God is all-sufficient. There is nothing we lack that He hasn't already made provision for. Life can get very difficult at times. Becoming the person God desires you to be can be met with great opposition in the form of family and friends, financial difficulty, relationship problems, lack of resources, emotional distress, physical problems, and more. But, in all this, God has made provisions through His grace to meet every one of our needs. It is His desire in our covenant relationship that we accept these provisions. This requires faith and trust in God. God is a Spirit. Therefore, realizing Him and His character requires a level of Spiritual faith and belief that He is real and that His character is to reward those who desire to walk in relationship with Him (Hebrews 11:6).

So many times, we look at life through our ability. That works if the issues we face fall under the purview of our resources or strengths. The stress of life occurs when our issues and problems become too much, and we find ourselves in way over our heads. We were never promised a life without problems, but we were promised a life above the circumstances. You are more than a conqueror. Your victory is in your relationship with God. In weakness, the best thing to do is to be honest with God. He already knows.

Unlike people, God doesn't use our weaknesses as a measurement tool. He is fully aware of every area of our lives. The void we have in our hearts was placed there by Him (Ecclesiastes 3:11). I have come to realize in my life that it's during the most uncomfortable times that I need God the most. I am constantly learning how to come to God as I am—not hiding my feelings, not hiding my fears, but relying on the reality of His unconditional love while learning to adore the beauty of His presence amid my weakness. I have to have faith in who He is and His character over my insecurities. When I give in to that faith, I see the power of unmerited grace at work, the healing that comes from transparency in the presence of the King. In those moments, I become aware of the Truth and realize that His presence and love is more than enough. He is more than enough for me. Somehow, at that moment, you forget the problem you had and begin to be submerged in the presence of the greatest force of life known to any man: the presence of God.

Beloved, when you get a revelation of God's great love, it makes the issues of this life very small.

The issue many times is that we allow the current experiences of life to diminish the power and joy only found in the presence of the King. Maybe we haven't achieved the level of life we desired, or our finances aren't the best; a relationship hasn't happened, or you were supposed to be married by this point. The truth of the matter is that regardless of what has or hasn't happened in life, God is bigger. His love for you is greater than anything you come against, and the power to overcome the feelings and thoughts you have are in His presence. Our weaknesses in the presence in the Lord are overcome by His unlimited power and strength. But God can't cover what we are not willing to reveal. The pains of life are real. What we experience is real. Yet God is more real. Therefore, we become people who are not afraid to speak of weaknesses in our life, because we know who covers every weakness with His perfect strength.

We were designed for a relationship with God. We were created to receive all that He is; to become everything He purposed us to be. The fear of failure is a great deceiver. Fear will drive us into pursuing another identity to hide from the Truth. It will cause us to hide. The truth of the matter is, within ourselves, we are all weak. In the public eye, we would all like to appear strong and perfect. In the social media eye, we would like to appear to have things all together and in perfect order, but, within our own ability, we have nothing. We are not enough within ourselves. We can't see beyond the moment that we are in. We do not have the power in ourselves to stop or overcome anything. We need a savior. All the money in the world could buy many things, but it cannot by a sound mind. We can have all the friends and associates and still not know the meaning of true love and purpose. These things can only be revealed by the source, God. We were designed to know life straight from the Father's heart to ours. The issues of life only prove that we are constantly in need of fellowship with Him. But if we are hiding from our frailty, then we deny ourselves the pleasure of seeing true deliverance.

It is a constant battle in the human mind to come to grips with the Truth that God is not afraid of our ugly past, our confused present, and the fears of what we think is an unknown future. Because He already knows the future. He is in the midst of it all, waiting to reveal the Truth of the matter. We must become determined to be real with God. I've heard it said this way: God can't heal the fake you. He can only heal the real you, the part of you that you will reveal. There is power in the word *forgive*, and one of the first people you need to forgive is yourself.

## Chapter 11

# It's Not Their Fault

**Matthew 18:20-21 (NKJV)**

**"'For where two or three are gathered together in My name, I am there in the midst of them.' Then Peter came to Him and said, 'Lord, how often shall my brother sin against me, and I forgive him? Up to seven times?'"**

The most powerful key to freedom is forgiveness. There is no greater liberation than coming into the knowledge that no one has the power to make you angry or keep you on the offense. I heard it said that forgiveness is a gift you give yourself. It seems odd because one would think that forgiveness is something you give your offender, but it is not. The reality is that when we hold people's wrongdoing in our hearts and mind, we place ourselves in prison. The person that hurt you, whether willingly or unwillingly, is no longer carrying the offense. As the offended party, you carry the weight of that situation. And if not released, it will take you down.

Jesus said in Matthew 6:15 (NIV), "But if you do not forgive others their sins, your Father will not forgive your sins." The truth is we have all sinned against someone, either in word or deed, but when we hurt another person, we actually sinned against God. But God in Christ forgave us. The scripture speaks to the freedom that is in forgiveness and the spiritual law that hurts us when we do not forgive. We nullify the work of Jesus on the cross, and the forgiveness of God is rendered powerless in our lives. The healing power that is released to forgiveness is overtaken by our fleshly desire to hold a grudge and to feel like we have the right to hold a grudge. The thought, "I deserve vindication," will keep us in bitterness, aggression, anger, strife, gossip, and covetousness. This spirit doesn't come from God.

Forgiveness is a gift you give yourself. God desires to keep you free. Jesus was explaining to His disciples the need to hold no record of wrongdoing, something the Apostle Paul would speak to in I Corinthians 13 when he talks about love. The power to forgive is rooted and grounded in agape love. This kind of love only comes by way of the Holy Spirit. Face it; we can't love unconditionally on our own. At our best, we can't love everyone all the time, regardless of what they do. Agape love is a perfect love, and God is the only one that can love perfectly. He gives us this gift through His Holy Spirit in our hearts.

Paul said in Romans 5:5 (NIV), "And hope does not put us to shame, because God's love has been poured out into our hearts through the Holy Spirit, who has been given to us." God has comforted us with perfect love to forgive people that have wronged us. Isn't that great news? But this love doesn't just take us over; it is something we must cultivate through reading, hearing, and speaking the Word of God and then by learning to obey the leading voice of the Holy Spirit.

Forgiving long term wounds will require a consistent and intentional effort to speak forgiveness to the person or persons that hurt you. You must build your faith in the area of forgiveness to receive the vision of seeing it the way God does. Know this: IT IS A PROCESS. It requires a committed faith in the Word of God.

A term that I've come to understand is: "Hurt people hurt people." I am not giving your offender a way out, but I am asking you to see the whole picture. Hurting people seek vindication and justice. When they don't get it based on their terms, they lash out. The people closest to them tend to get it the worse. Some have been exposed or have been raised in a culture of abuse and only know one way to communicate or relate to others, and that is through using and abusing others. The source of this behavior is not natural; it is spiritual.

Jesus spoke these words on the day of His crucifixion. "Jesus said, 'Father, forgive them, for they do not know what they are doing'" (Luke 23:34). One would think these Words were misspoken. The people who nailed Jesus on the cross after flogging, slapping, punching, and spitting on Him, all while ridiculing Him, had to be fully aware of their words and deeds. But their action was birthed out of an evil heart and mind. That idea didn't come from them; it came from the devil. He planned to destroy Jesus; he used people to do it.

The Jews really didn't understand that what they were doing was sinning against the Son of God. Can

I let you in on another gospel truth? You are a Son of God as well. "Beloved, now we are children of God; and it has not yet been revealed what we shall be, but we know that when He is revealed, we shall be like Him, for we shall see Him as He is. " (1 John 3:2 NKJV). You were made in the image and likeness of God. When we hurt one another, we hurt God. Therefore, when we hurt one another, it's like spinning against God. Yet God FORGAVE! If he can do it for us, then we can do it for others. Believe me: if they realized that you were made in the image of God, they would not have tried to crucify you with their words or actions. The best thing to do is to let them go!

Your forgiveness may be painful right now, but on the other side of your pain is the salvation of many people. Know this love is powerful. It covers a multitude of sins, and it can't die. Be healed of the bitterness and grief. Be delivered from the pride of wanting to be right. Submit to the will of God and speak the words, "I forgive."

If Jesus didn't forgive His persecutors, He wouldn't be the Resurrected Lord today. He is the perfect theology—an example of what God desires from our human lives. Forgiveness is a gift you give yourself. Let it go and make strides to press on. You may never get an apology. Let God become your vindicator. Settle the matter with the Father and keep living your life. God has a way of touches people's hearts, but He can't do it if you're trying to do His job. Instead of telling everyone you can about the horrible incident, cast the care on the Lord. Prayer is the most powerful key to connecting to the heart of God. Freedom is a gift from God, and it's impossible to experience with forgiveness. So, let's pray!

*Chapter 12*

# I Need Comfort

**John 14:16 Amplified Bible Classic Edition (AMPC)**

**"And I will ask the Father, and He will give you another Comforter (Counselor, Helper, Intercessor, Advocate, Strengthener, and Standby), that He may remain with you forever—"**

God always desires to deliver us from the things that try to overcome us. As I stated in the last chapter, God is not able to deliver us from something we will not reveal. Though He is sovereign, God will not violate your will. We must submit our will to His will to see His desire fulfilled in our lives. The things we are not willing to reveal will manifest in other areas of our lives. We will find comfort in other things. We were designed with a dependency gap. We were not created to produce life out of our being. Our life flows from the Spirit of God. Outside of the spirit, we are nothing.

Jesus, in John 14:16, refers to the Holy Spirit as the comforter. Have you ever been cold in the winter? I remember as a child going to bed in the wintertime and laying down in my bed. The sheets cold and the chill that would hit my body from the bed. It was as if the sheets I had were not enough to do the job. Well, in the summer, those sheets were more than adequate. I didn't need much coverage during that season. But as the temperature dropped, there was a need for more. My natural sense picked up on the idea that what I had was no longer enough to keep me secure.

I remember my mother bringing in a thicker blanket. It was weighty and filled with more substance than the thinner sheets on the bed. This thicker, weightier covering was known as a comforter. Under this comforter, I was able to get the heat needed to enjoy my rest. In life, we all go through seasons, and every season requires different support to accomplish the desired end. No one desires to have a failed life. We all desire to succeed and be an asset to the world around us. But when things get uncomfortable, we need comforting. The Holy Spirit is the agent that God has given us to overcome the weaknesses in our lives. When we reveal the weaknesses in our lives to God, it is His Holy Spirit that helps us navigate to the place of deliverance and healing that is needed. When we try to fix things outside of the Spirit of God, we begin to rely on natural things to comfort us. Sex, drugs, food, sleep, money, and television are a few areas in which I have tried in the past to find comfort. The Word of God says in John 6:63 (NIV): **"The Spirit gives life; the flesh counts for nothing. The words I have spoken to you—they are full of the Spirit and life."**

*I Need Comfort*

We all have proclivities to natural comforts. They seem to make sense: the things that tried to plague our lives in the natural appeal to our flesh. The issues we may have had in a relationship could manifest in eating disorders or "retail therapy." We try to locate a means of justifying negative emotions by seeking euphoria through a natural means. Or, maybe it's having sex with multiple partners or just having sex for comforting a broken place in your heart and mind. The seasons of life bring out different elements of need in our lives, but what I desire to reveal to you, dear reader is that there is no natural answer for a broken heart. You can't eat enough ice cream to heal a deep-seated wound in the heart. Money can't replace the years that you lost without a mother or a father. Sex can't replace the abuse you suffered. These are areas that God has given His Spirit to heal.

The flesh counts for nothing. Consider that thought. Jesus speaks very clearly in this passage. There isn't a natural answer to a persistent problem. Eternity is in the Spirit. I know you may be thinking that the pain you feel happened to you in the natural. And yes, you are correct. But the pain you feel is a result of a broken heart and mind that will not allow you to forget. The image of what took place still rings in your mind. The depths of your being despises the day it happened, and every sense—smell, sound, taste, sight, and touch—remind you of the experience. While the event has passed, the spirit of depression, shame, and condemnation have moved in. These are spiritual enemies. You can't touch depression. But the spirit of depression speaks. The thought of shame sounds loud. The voice of condemnation roars as if it were a dangerous lion. These things can't be eliminated by natural means.

It is going to take the Word of God through the power of the Holy Spirit to heal from every traumatic experience. The Spirit gives life; Jesus makes this very clear, also. The Spirit of God is total life. There is no depression in God. Can I let you in on a big secret? God is not ashamed of you, and He is not condemning you! The voice of condemnation and shame comes from the forces of darkness: Satan and his army. To defeat the lie that comes against you, you must realize the truth. Truth will never be defeated by a lie. Truth always prevails. So, the Spirit leads to life. What kind of life exactly? The life of God. The life God planned for you.

The bumps along the journey of life try to get us off track. The traumatic experiences, the moments that feel like the epic fail, the big disappointments—these natural occurrences are ploys to take your eyes off the bigger picture. The bigger picture is what God has placed inside of you. This beautiful gift was meant to touch the world and bring positive change that would reflect the goodness of God to all people. We were never made to be selfish; we were designed by God to be selfless as He is.

When we experience negative things in our lives, it causes us to judge ourselves outside of God's insight (the Spirit of the Word). We base the encounter on natural terms, things we have already seen or heard in this fallen world. These experiences, if not taken to God with transparency, will file themselves in our consciousness, creating strongholds. *Stronghold* is an old word that speaks to a fortified place. It's a war term; men would build them so that the enemy couldn't get in and overtake them. Strongholds in the mind are the enemies who use the mind against you by hiding in the crevices of our thought life until the perfect moment when they spring forth negative emotions and feelings. As I stated earlier, in the presence of God, these weaknesses can be torn down. Just as Joshua and the armies of Israel shouted down the walls of Jericho, so can you, by the Spirit of the living God, tear down the strongholds in your mind and take back the life that God has purposed for you.

God has given you a precious gift in His Holy Spirit. There is nothing in this life that He doesn't already have the answer to. He is the Spirit of Grace. Our lives were meant to work in partnership with Him. He is our guide through life. Like the blanket my mother brought me in the winter season, He is our comforter. He makes us secure. Unlike many of the things we try to use for relief, the Holy Spirit is eternal. Things like sex and drugs only give temporary pleasure; you are never able to go to what is needed to reach the next level, so you are always tempted to try something else riskier. The Holy Spirit is not risky. He is life and life more abundantly. The Holy Spirit can handle all our natural proclivities. He works on us from the inside out, realigning our eternal being and then landscaping the outside until we begin to look like Jesus.

It's work; it's a process. It takes time, but when you yield to the Word and the Spirit, you begin to see the person God sees and not the events that have scarred you in life. Your comfort and help become more recognizable, and you can resist the urge and need to depend on natural elements for comfort. It should be our desire to receive every gift that God promised us. The Holy Spirit is the most precious gift that He gave after the Lord Jesus Christ. The Spirit is the down payment on our glorified life. We must allow the Holy Spirit to search our hearts and minds to reveal the secrets hidden from us so that we can reveal them openly before God and heal. Forgiveness is a major factor in the process.

*Chapter 13*

# The Real Conversation With God

**Psalm 139:23-24 (NIV)**

**"Search me, God, and know my heart;
test me and know my anxious thoughts.
See if there is any offensive way in me
and lead me in the way everlasting."**

The beauty of the Holy Spirit is spoken about in this amazing passage of scripture: a desire in the heart of David made a request to God. Search me. That's an amazing request to the sovereign God, who already knows the hearts of men. Yet David, from his pursuit, said God, search my human heart. There must have been things in there that David knew were not the best, yet there was a great love and need for the Father.

The things in our hearts can, many times, seem hidden. We know that a part of us is lacking, and there is a void. But the thing that keeps us out of the flow of

God's presence is an issue. Maybe they are things that we have allowed to take God's priority in our lives. The truth is, we can get so comfortable with social media, cars, clothes, shoes, relationships, money, and status that we become dull to the fact that our desire for God has become cold. So sometimes the request in prayer must be, Search my heart. How does He search my heart? Hebrews 4:12 (KJV) "For the word of God is quick, and powerful, and sharper than any two-edged sword, piercing even to the dividing asunder of soul and spirit, and the joints and marrow, and is a discerner of the thoughts and intents of the heart."

The first level of understanding and searching the heart is found in the Word of God. To receive a spiritual conviction, we must be a hearer of the Word of Truth. God's Truth far surpasses human knowledge. And Jesus told us in John 17:17 as He was speaking to the Father, "Sanctify them by thy truth, Your Word is your Truth." The Truth brings light, and light illuminates the darkness, even dark things hidden in our hearts. Hebrews 4:12 says that the Word is quick, as I would interpret it means alive, sensitive to life, and able to interpret life at life speed no matter the generation or time. The scripture goes on to say that it is a discerner of the thoughts and intentions of the heart.

The Word of God will help us realize what's right and wrong about our hearts. Simply reading or hearing the Word of God begins the process of searching the inward parts of the heart and magnifies what Truth is and what is a lie, what is of God and what is worldly. It reveals what comes from the Spirit of Life and what comes from the spirit of death. It begins to center its focus on who or what is Lord of your life. When I read the Word, I always read it with an open heart. I try to be cognizant of my own condition and remember that God's Word is always right, regardless of what passage I am reading. When I read things that I am currently not doing, I am immediately faced with a decision. Obey and repent or disobey and disregard what I just saw. Either way, the truth has come, and it is up to me to decide whether I am going to walk in it or not.

### 1 Corinthians 2:10-12 (NLT)

> "But it was to us that God revealed these things by his Spirit. For his, Spirit searches out everything and shows us God's deep secrets. No one can know a person's thoughts except that person's spirit, and no one can know God's thoughts except God's own Spirit. And we have received God's Spirit (not the world's spirit), so we can know the wonderful things God has freely given us."

Isn't it good to know that God doesn't charge us for wisdom and advice? The second measure of searching the heart comes by way of the Holy Spirit; this is the Spirit that comes from God. He is God's representation to you—your Helper. He operates solely on the Word of God the Father, and He teaches us to live like God the Son. It's a powerful chemistry once you begin to get the revelation of it. God desires to lead you back to the person He purposed you to be.

*The Transparent Life & Your Eternal Destiny*

**Learning to Trust Again**

Being led is not a process we naturally pick up, especially being led by a Spirit we cannot see. But truth be told, we were unfortunately led by a spirit before Christ. That spirit was a spirit of darkness. That spirit was rebellious, disrespectful, selfish, self-righteous, a liar, a thief—and the horrible list goes on and on. We were all in some way found in this condition by God. And He sent His Son into the world to save us from ourselves.

The worst critic we have in life is ourselves. No one is harder on us than we are on ourselves. This trait wasn't yours at birth. You were trained to think this way by a broken culture and a society of people without a close relationship with God, the Father, and the Word of His Spirit. The enemy of this world blinded the minds of people by trying to keep us away from unconditional love and faith in the Father. See I Corinthians 4:3-5. Coming to Christ was an amazing miracle.

For some, we see instant deliverance from major addictions and bad life cycles, but the days after are filled with one relapse after another. Before you allow condemnation to creep in, please know God hasn't stopped loving you. He hasn't given up on you. His blood still flows in your direction to cleanse you. Trust and believe.

I desire to let you know that salvation is a journey, and you must learn how to trust God; this is a relationship that will never end until we are glorified on the last day. God, by His Word and His Spirit, wants to deconstruct our way of thinking and restore us into the perfect image of His Son. This process will not be perfect, but as you trust God's Word over your feelings,

*The Real Conversation With God*

you will see that He is right there with you every step of the way. He does this because He loves you. Unlike natural Fathers, God's love is pure. It's built on no conditions outside of the one He made with Jesus: to die so that the whole world could receive salvation and the forgiveness of sins through Him. It is through the repetitive hearing and walking out the Word of God that we see His unwavering faithfulness.

The Father has a way of truly blowing our minds when we acknowledge His presence and realize that He was there all along. We begin to know that He will NEVER leave us or forsake us. Trust is not given it is earned. God knows this, and He has done everything possible to earn your trust. The whole work of salvation is His resume, to take back the job of being your total provision source. The Bible is His book of work experiences, and the prophets, judges, and kings are all references with Jesus being the greatest reference of the Father's outstanding, radical love. This love must be first received before it can manifest itself to help you live, and it will not manifest if you never begin to work the levels of trust.

Trust is relational. You will never give trust to someone you do not know. Knowing someone is a very intimate and intentional word. You don't know someone intimately by accident. It may not have been planned, but getting to know them was a choice. Whether tentative at first or all in, once you felt comfortable, you opened to the other person, and they were able to open to you. You began to see things about them that were not noticeable on the surface; there was more to them. As time went on, you saw they were faithful to keep your most intimate detail and respect your integrity. They were a great support to your dreams and plans and encouraged you to press on when times got tough. They gave you the things you needed when you didn't have the resources to get them, and they were always a listening ear and gave sound advice when it was needed. Someone like this in the natural would be considered an amazing friend. Well, this has been the character of God all the time. He desires to show you how faithful He can be to you. But you must stay in the process.

## Chapter 14

# Love's Got You

**Romans 2:4 NIV**

**"Or do you show contempt for the riches of his kindness, forbearance and patience, not realizing that God's kindness is intended to lead you to repentance?"**

Let God love you into submission. God already knows everything there is to know about you. Yet He still calls for a personal relationship with you. Not so that He can get better acquainted with you, but so that you can get better acquainted with Him. And in knowing Him, you can get to know yourself better. When God, who is love searches us by way of His Word and His Holy Spirit, we realize things about our past and present and the hope for our future. It's God's Spirit that communicates to our human spirit that we are His children (Romans 8:16).

God is love! A powerful statement that would seem simple, but honestly, it isn't, because we have created so many definitions of love that the actual divine meaning of the word has been diluted down to human affection. But, as we have stated before, God is not a man. Therefore, His love is far greater; in all honesty, it is not even on the same level for comparison. We must leave our knowledge of love to embrace the love of God fully. Love God's way is known as *agape*. Agape, in its Greek meaning, is love or goodwill. This kind of love is eternal love because it flows straight from the source of eternity Himself, and He doesn't change. This kind of love is the love that God has for the whole world (John 3:16-18). God loved the whole world, including you and I, when we were in sin. He loved us when we knowingly chose other options of comfort over His eternal presence. His love never overlooked us or cast us away. His love came up with the plan to deliver us all through Jesus Christ.

God's love will never look at you for your past mistakes because He sees you like He sees His perfect Son. This is a revelation that requires faith to receive. For many of us, myself included, we have had such a distorted idea of love that the thought of someone loving us without conditions attached seems utter foolishness. No one loves perfectly, but God does.

**1 Peter 4:8 (NIV)**

**"Above all, love each other deeply, because love covers over a multitude of sins."**

Love is the most powerful force known to man. One simple act of love can change a person's life. It has the power to heal. God's love transcends all deficiencies. Consider Jesus; He never met a person that He wouldn't heal. None of them were born again. They weren't all devoted Bible readers. They didn't fit the criteria that we base perfection on. They were the least, the overlooked, the downcast. The people that the Pharisees and Sadducees would call sinners. These are the people that Christ did notable miracles for. Why? Because of the great compassion, He had for all humankind. This is the Love of the Father. Jesus is perfect theology. He models the will of God in the flesh perfectly. He turned no one away that came to Him in faith. This brings a great truth to bear; faith works by love.

Galatians 5:6 (NIV) reads, "For in Christ Jesus, neither circumcision nor uncircumcision has any value. The only thing that counts is faith expressing itself through love." Faith is the force that receives what God has for you, but love is the force that causes us to reach for the promise. To know the love of God brings hope into our lives because we see that God has an unconditional, unlimited amount of love for us. This love never runs out. It is authored and finished in the perfect work of Jesus.

Beloved, I pray you begin to see with the eyes of faith a love for you that will never leave you, no matter how bad your life gets, or bad your decisions become, the Love of God is greater. You simply must believe in it. In our natural lives, we are taught to believe it when you see it. In the realm of the spirit, you are taught to believe it, then you will see it. God's love will grow in you; the more you simply place yourself into an environment to hear. Faith comes by hearing the Word of God. To realize God's perfect love, listen for it. The more you hear about His love, the stronger your ability to believe in His love becomes. You can't truly come to the knowledge of something you have not first heard. Life itself will try to convince you that the issues in your life and the mistakes you have made have separated you from God. But here is what God's word says in Romans 8:31 (NIV): "What then shall we say to these things? If God *is* for us, who *can be* against us?"

God is for you, not against you. Later in verses 38-39, Paul says, "For I am convinced that neither death nor life, neither angels nor demons, neither the present nor the future, nor any powers, neither height nor depth, nor anything else in all creation, will be able to separate us from the love of God that is in Christ Jesus our Lord."

God has sealed you with his love. He is totally committed to you. He has committed his unchanging Word to you, and He has sealed you with His Holy Spirit. Don't allow the trials of life to separate you in your mind from God's unfailing love. Nothing you are going through has alienated you from the presence of God. His Spirit is with you right now, waiting on you to acknowledge Him. I believe with you now that you will experience His comforting presence all around you. I pray that you find assurance in the Father's love. When all other things fade away, know that the Father's love remains. No matter what you are facing in life, it is God who will cause you to triumph through Christ Jesus!

*Chapter 15*

# More Than a Conqueror

**2 Corinthians 2:14 (NKJV)**

**"Now thanks *be* to God who always leads us in triumph in Christ, and through us diffuses the fragrance of His knowledge in every place."**

You were born to be a winner in life, and victory has been perfected in Christ. No matter the issue or circumstance, Christ has defeated it in the flesh, crucified it, and rose again so that you and I can come to the knowledge of this salvation and never again give in to the temptation to quit or give in to past weaknesses. You and I are captives of Christ; He has won us through His victory over death, hell, and the grave. We were destined for hell due to our transgressions. We were slaves to the lust and the weaknesses of our flesh, but Christ came in the flesh and overcame all the works of the flesh and redeemed us. He bought us back. Our purpose was lost and our destiny was destruction. But

God, through Christ, gave us hope and a future. This future came to us by grace. We received victory in a war we didn't even have to fight in. We overcame the enemy of this world through Christ Jesus. You have already overcome your situation right now. Will you believe that? Will you say it?

Your life is now meant to be lived by faith in the Son of God (Galatians 2:20). Each day brings new challenges; the key to living as an overcomer is to remember who you are in Christ. The enemy will try his very best to get you to fall back into your old life, but you overcome him by resisting him. **James 4:7-8 (NKJV) "Therefore submit to God. Resist the devil and he will flee from you. Draw near to God and He will draw near to you. Cleanse *your* hands, *you* sinners; and purify *your* hearts, *you* double-minded."**

Please know this truth: the devil has no authority in your life. If you have made Christ your Lord, then you have inherited His life and everything that comes with it. That includes His victory over the enemy. You are not a product of your environment. You do not have to live with fear as a victim. You just need to keep the constant reminder of who you are in Christ. The scripture in James tells us to submit to God. *Submit* means to subordinate, or to place yourself under subjection. When we submit to God, we place ourselves under the subjection of God's word concerning us. Whatever He said becomes the final authority. God's Word becomes your standing power. His word gives you the fortitude to stand the more you give yourself to it. The Word of God will redefine you when you truly make it the center of your focus. The lies and plots of the enemy become powerless when you realize that they never had grounds to take you down. This is a fight that will be fought every day. Devotion is a practice that strengthens you in your faith.

The only way to overcome the enemy is in the arena of faith. The enemy does not want you to have faith because he knows that if you get a clue about who God made you to be, he would never be able to stop you again. Jesus told it to us in a parable this way: "When anyone hears the word of the Kingdom and does not understand *it,* then the wicked *one* comes and snatches away what was sown in his heart; this is he who received seed by the wayside" (Matthew 13:19, NKJV).

God wants you to win-win over addictions; win over poverty; win over slothfulness; win over abuse, and win over rejection. The power that brings you out is a constant dedication to the Word of God. The only way we can resist the tormenting thoughts of the enemy and fears is to yield to the Word of God and renew our mind to His will over the way we feel.

**Romans 8:31-37 (NKJV)**

**"What then shall we say to these things? If God *is* for us, who *can be* against us? He who did not spare His own Son, but delivered Him up for us all, how shall He not with Him also freely give us all things? Who shall bring a charge against God's elect? *It is* God who justifies. Who *is* he who condemns? *It is* Christ who died, and furthermore is also risen, who is even at the right hand of God, who also makes intercession for us. Who shall separate us from**

**the love of Christ? *Shall* tribulation, or distress, or persecution, or famine, or nakedness, or peril, or sword? As it is written:**

**"For Your sake we are killed all day long;**

**We are accounted as sheep for the slaughter."**

**Yet in all these things we are more than conquerors through Him who loved us."**

I know sometimes it seems as if the voice in your head is telling you this is just the way it was meant to be. That you just have to live with it. These thoughts are the words of the enemy trying to get you to buy into his desires and lies. They are trying to condemn you, but God is not condemning you. He has forgiven you; therefore, your victory is in knowing that you're free from condemnation (Romans 8:1). You are more than a conqueror. Nothing can bind you up when you know how God sees you and how He feels about you. Don't allow the lies of this world, and the words from other people place you back into the bondage of your past. God has set you up in Christ to win.

You were born with great promise. You are who you are because God needed you to be exactly that. You are uniquely placed in the time you are to make an impact on the world around you. Don't get distracted. Go back to the Father, find your direction from the One that called you. The task may appear daunting at times, but know this God is for you, and you were created for moments like this. Take joy in the test, and place your faith in God's perfect will for your life. You will never lose in the arena of faith. Keep walking in your gift, and don't compare. Grow through mistakes and learn something at each turn. You are becoming. Don't give up. You are called for such a time as this. Make today another intentional day to live, love, and grow.

www.ingramcontent.com/pod-product-compliance
Ingram Content Group UK Ltd.
Pitfield, Milton Keynes, MK11 3LW, UK
UKHW022210230426
12048UKWH00016BA/768